the city

Translation: Jean Grasso Fitzpatrick

First English language edition published
1986 by Barron's Educational Series, Inc.

© Parramón Ediciones, S.A., 1986

The title of the Spanish edition is *la ciudad*

All rights reserved.
No part of this book may be reproduced in any form, by photostat, microfilm, xerography, or other means, or incorporated into any information retrieval system, electronic or mechanical, without the written permission of the copyright owner.

All inquiries should be addressed to:
Barron's Educational Series, Inc.
113 Crossways Park Drive
Woodbury, New York 11797
Library of Congress Catalog Card No. 86-8015

International Standard Book No.
Paper: 0-8120-3700-6
Hardcover: 0-8120-5748-1

Library of Congress Cataloging-in-Publication Data

Rius, María.
    Let's discover the city.

    (Let's discover series)
    Translation of: *La Ciudad*.
    Summary: Explains the evolution of the city, its good and bad points, and ways we can make it more comfortable.
    1. Cities and towns—History—Juvenile literature. 2. City and town life—Juvenile literature.
    [1. Cities and towns. 2. City and town life]
    I. Parramón, José María. II. Title.
    HT111.R5413 1986   307.7'64   86-8015
    ISBN 0-8120-5748-1
    ISBN 0-8120-3700-6 (pbk.)

Printed in Spain
by Gráficas Estella, S.A.
Estella (Navarra)
Register Book Number: 785
Legal Deposit: NA-182-1986

let's discover
the city

María Rius
J. M. Parramón

Woodbury, New York • Toronto

When you go out of your house, you see houses—many houses!

When you are in the street, you see people—many people!

and traffic lights, and signs, and big billboards…

When you hear the fire engines pass...
and hear horns honking...

and see wide avenues and beautiful monuments.

When you pass tall, tall buildings…

and see windows, and more windows…

and there are parks where you can play.

When you are in a place where there are many different neighborhoods,

and at night there are only lights, and people, and more lights.

When you see blue haze in the air....

THE CITY

GUIDE FOR PARENTS AND TEACHERS

*City-dwellers—
We are also the landscape
of the city.
You, you and I,
we are one, we are two, we are three.
We are a people, you know?*

Gil Cabestany

The urban landscape

Cities were built by people. Just look out any window of any house in any city. Everything you see—buildings, houses, cars, train stations—everything was built by people, and, along with the constant movement of all those people coming and going, these things form what we call the urban landscape.

How cities began

Cities began with the discovery of agriculture. When people could grow their own food on farms, in addition to hunting and fishing, they forgot their wandering and nomadic way of life. They decided to settle down in groups. When people were all together they probably felt safer. But more than that, together they could share their lives and the work that had to be done. Out of all this sharing came the first village, which continued to grow through the centuries to become the city.

Evolution of the city

From the moment people started living together, they started establishing rules and community services that made life in a group possible. This made their homes and lives more comfortable and safer. The city continued to grow until the Middle Ages. Then, for protection, it moved within the walls around a castle or monastery. There, people with different talents—such as weavers and potters—decided to form groups called guilds. Since weavers need bowls and potters need cloth, trade and commerce began to develop. This way of life didn't change for about a thousand years. Then the Industrial Revolution, with its machines and big factories, started in the eighteenth and nineteenth centuries. Many people came to the city from farms in the countryside to work in the new factories. That changed the way the city was arranged and run. The small cities grew bigger and bigger until they became what we know today. Around the ancient part of the city—made of low houses and narrow winding streets—new districts were built with tall buildings and wider streets. The wide streets made it possible for many cars, and buses, and trolleys to carry people where they needed to go. The small towns around the edges of the city were soon surrounded, and they formed all the different neighborhoods and suburbs that make up the great cities of today.

Good things and bad things about the city

Today, the city gives us many things. As it was in the beginning, the city is still a place where people find it easiest to meet other people, make friends, and work together. The city gives us things to do during our free time, whether we visit parks and gardens, sports stadiums, movies, or the theater. The city also offers us many cultural and educational opportunities at its many schools, libraries, universities, concert halls, scientific laboratories, and museums.

The bad things? Yes, there are those, too. The neighborhoods often grow too quickly, there is too much traffic, and the air is often dirty—pollution made by factory fumes and automobile exhaust. This makes life in the city very uncomfortable at times. But, remember that people made the city, and if we made the city, we can always change it to make it a better place to live.

Civic awareness and urban planning

To make our big cities less uncomfortable, people have tried two solutions: make city dwellers aware of the problems, and make them proud of themselves and their neighborhoods. The city government, headed by the mayor, is in charge of keeping everything running smoothly. The city officials organize campaigns to keep people safe, set up special traffic rules, rules for taking care of pets, and rules for making sure the people stay healthy—a whole set of rules that enable city dwellers to live together happily, sharing the work of running the city smoothly. Also, urban planning lets people study the way the city grew and developed so they can take care of new needs without changing the original neighborhoods, or the way people like to live together. That way, each city can keep its special areas, its unique beauty, its different traditions, and also keep all its people happy.

Each city is different, in its size, in its structure, in its history, but all have something in common that defines them as cities: their inhabitants do not dedicate themselves to agricultural work, but to other professions in commerce, industry, or the world of culture. Furthermore, they live with the continual stimulation of the advantages and attractions offered by modern life.